60p

6
MINUTE
MORNING
THIGHS & HIPS

6 MINUTE MORNING
THIGHS & HIPS

SARA ROSE

Bath · New York · Singapore · Hong Kong · Cologne · Delhi · Melbourne

This edition published by Parragon in 2009

Parragon
Queen Street House
4 Queen Street
Bath BA1 1HE, UK

ISBN: 978-1-4075-7233-8

Printed in Malaysia

Created and produced by Ivy Contract
Photography: Ian Parsons
Model: Jade

The views expressed in this book are those of the author but they are general
views only and readers are urged to consult a relevant and qualified specialist for
individual advice in particular situations. Parragon hereby excludes all liability to
the extent permitted by law for any errors or omissions in this book and for any
loss, damage or expense (whether direct or indirect) suffered by a third party
relying on any information contained in this book.

Ivy Contract would like to thank Getty Images for permission to reproduce
copyright material on pages 6 (Ray Kachatorian/Taxi), 7 (Safia Fatimi/Photonica).

Caution
Please check with your doctor/therapist before attempting this workout,
particularly if you are suffering from an injury, are pregnant or have just had a
baby. It is recommended that new mothers wait at least six weeks post partum
before participating in exercise (12 weeks if it was a Caesarean birth). If you
feel any pain or discomfort at any point, please stop exercising immediately and
seek medical advice.

CONTENTS

INTRODUCTION

Covered up and out of sight for most of the year, the hips and thighs are usually the areas of the body that need the most work. But if you hate the idea of living in the gym or becoming a diet-book bore, don't despair. Just try out the quick and easy routines in this book and you'll have streamlined hips and leaner thighs sooner than you think.

Great reasons for shaping up

Apart from the obvious benefit of improving your appearance, firming and toning up your hips and thighs is actually good for your health. Strengthening your hip and thigh muscles will improve your balance and posture, and increase your flexibility, helping to keep your body in tip-top condition as you get older. As an added bonus, you'll find it easier to control your weight, because muscles burn more calories than fat.

Morning exercise

For most people exercising in the morning is best, when you are refreshed after a night's sleep. Your body is very receptive to exercise

in the morning – since it tends to be done on an empty stomach, it forces your body to use its fat reserves. Exercising at this time also kick-starts your metabolism and helps keep you burning calories throughout the day.

The workout space

You will need an uncluttered space that is warm and well-ventilated. Ideally, there will be enough space to enable you to take at least five steps in all directions. An exercise mat is a good idea to cushion your body when doing floor work. If possible, try to do your exercise routine in front of a full-length mirror so that you can keep an eye on what you are doing.

What to wear

Wear several layers of comfortable clothing as you start to exercise to warm up your muscles, and gradually strip off some of these layers as you get warmer. Clothes should be loose, soft and made from a breathable fabric – shorts and a vest covered with jogging bottoms and a sweatshirt, for example, are ideal.

How to use this book

The key to fabulously toned thighs and hips is to exercise little but often. This book has a series of easy exercises that are designed to fit into 6-minute programmes, enabling you to slot a workout into even your busiest day. Exercises are grouped into suggested programmes at the end of the book, but you can mix and match your own for even more variety. Building muscle tone doesn't happen overnight, but the beauty of these short routines is that you won't become bored or burned out. Keep it up and you'll find that just 6 minutes a day really will make a difference.

YOU AND YOUR BODY

Before you embark on an exercise routine, it is very helpful to have a basic understanding of how your body works, and why it's important to have good posture. Being muscle-aware will help you target the areas you want to firm up.

How your body moves

Your body's framework is the skeleton, made up of more than 200 bones that support your body and allow you to move. Muscles fixed to the ends of bones permit an enormous range of movement. However, joints and muscles that aren't regularly exercised become stiff and immobile, leading to pain and possible injury.

Muscles are made up of millions of tiny protein filaments that relax and contract to produce movement. Most muscles are attached to bones by tendons and are consciously controlled by your brain. Movement happens when muscles pull on tendons, which move the bones at the joints.

Most movements require the use of several muscle groups. In this book, you will be working a particular set of muscles for streamlined hips and thighs (see below).

All about posture

Good posture results from your spine maintaining its natural curve, without arching or sagging. If your posture is incorrect, every movement you make will be inefficient, leading to tiredness, weakness, aching joints and muscles and an increased risk of injury. Test your posture by standing on one leg – you should be able to balance without wobbling! The good news is that toning the muscles to trim the hips and thighs will naturally improve your posture, because these muscles balance the hip area.

Back of body

BUTTOCKS: there are three buttock muscles – gluteus maximus (the biggest muscle in the body), medius and minimus. They hold your pelvis in position, stabilize your hips and balance the hip area. Buttock muscles help keep you upright and pull your legs back as you walk. If you spend a lot of time sitting down they're likely to be slack and flabby!
HAMSTRINGS: these are three long muscles below the buttock muscles, which run from the back of the hipbone to the back of the knee. The hamstrings work with the gluteus maximus to bend your knee and rotate your hips.

Front of body

HIP FLEXORS: a group of muscles that run from the hips to the spine and from various points along the thighbone. They include the adductors (inner thigh muscles) and abductors (outer thigh muscles). They work in opposition to the buttock muscles, helping you to move your hips, and lift your thighs and knees.
QUADRICEPS: four muscles that run down the front of the thigh that enable you to extend your legs and bend your hips.

Before you get started

Warming up is very important – if you don't warm up you are likely to injure yourself because your muscles, tendons and ligaments will be taut. The 6-minute routines assume that you will have warmed up beforehand – this can be as simple as running on the spot for a few minutes followed by some stretches.

Just as important as warming up before exercising is cooling down afterward. As well as helping to prevent dizziness and a sudden drop in body temperature, cooling down realigns working muscles to their normal position in order to avoid tightness and stiffness.

Reps and sets

Muscle-building exercises are done as a series of repetitions (reps). One repetition equals one exercise. A set is a group of repetitions and usually consists of anything between 6 and 12 reps. The aim of repeating exercises is to work until your muscles feel tired, and over time this will strengthen them so that they can work even harder. It's important that you don't stop for more than a minute between exercises. Shorter recovery periods result in better muscles all round and improved muscle endurance. So keep going!

A hip and thigh diet?

For slimmer thighs and hips follow a low-fat diet in addition to your toning and shaping routines.
- Trim all visible fat off meat.
- Steam or grill food rather than frying or boiling
- Fill up with carbohydrates that release their energy slowly e.g. wholegrain pasta, rice, cereals
- Eat plenty of fresh fruit and vegetables.
- Drink plenty of water. This will flush out toxins from your body that can cause the appearance of dimpled flesh on your thighs.
- Steer clear of salty foods – they promote water retention in all parts of your body.

Breathing

The correct way to breathe when exercising is breathe in slowly through your nose (notice how your abdominal cavity rises as you do so), and breathe out slowly through your mouth. Make sure you continue to breathe in and out regularly throughout. And don't hold your breath – this will cause blood pressure to rise, which can be dangerous.

Cold muscles and joints are less flexible and more prone to strain so you must warm up before doing your exercise routine to make your movements safer. The following pages have some exercise ideas to warm up your hip and thigh muscles, but you could always devise your own. Remember to include some stretches after you've warmed up your muscles.

3

Marching on the spot

This is a quick and easy way to raise your body temperature and increase blood flow to the muscles. March on the spot for at least a minute. Swing your arms and gradually raise your knees higher as you go, and keep your breathing deep and regular.

Hip circles

Try this exercise to warm up your pelvic muscles. Keep your torso still — only your pelvis should be moving.

1 Stand up straight with your knees slightly bent, feet hip-width apart, and your hands resting on your hips.

2 Gently draw in your navel towards your spine to tighten your abdominal muscles. Do not suck in your waist or hold your breath — this movement should feel light and subtle.

3 Slowly circle your pelvis to the right so that you are rotating in a full circle.

4 Repeat nine times to the right then circle ten times to the left.

Knee bends

This exercise loosens the hip flexor muscles and helps warm up all the leg muscles. Don't lock your knees as you do this, and bend only as far as is comfortable.

1 Stand with one hand resting on a support such as a high-backed chair or a table, your feet hip-width apart and slightly turned out. Tighten your abdominal muscles.

2 Slowly bend your knees and lower your hips, then straighten up again. Use your buttock and leg muscles to lower and straighten.

3 Repeat nine times.

2

WATCH POINT
Never point your toes inwards while exercising – this can damage your knees.

2

Leg swings

This exercise warms up the hip joints. Don't swing your legs too high (about 45 degrees is high enough), and keep the movements controlled and flowing.

1 Stand with one hand resting on a support, such as a high-backed chair or a table, and balance on one leg with the knee slightly bent. Tighten your stomach muscles to protect your back.

2 Gently swing your other leg forward and backward. Keep your hips still as your leg moves from back to front. Swing up to 20 times on one leg then swap sides and swing on the other leg.

Standing knee lift

This exercise mobilizes the quadriceps and the hip flexors at the front of your body.

1 Stand up straight with your left hand on a chair to balance you.

2 Tighten your abdominal muscles.

3 Pull up your right knee so that your foot is parallel to your left knee.

4 Release and repeat on the other leg.

5 Repeat nine more times on each leg.

Standing leg circles

This exercise warms up the buttock muscles by lifting and drawing them together.

1 Stand up straight with good posture with your knees soft and legs hip-width apart. For balance hold on to a chair.

2 Tighten your abdominal muscles by gently pulling in your navel towards your backbone.

3 Lift your left leg a few inches off the floor and gently circle it one way, then the other.

4 Return to the starting position and repeat on the other leg.

5 Repeat nine more times on each leg.

3

3

Standing quad (front of thigh) stretch

1 Stand up straight with your feet hip-width apart and your knees soft (slightly bent). Tighten your stomach muscles to protect your back.

2 Bend one leg up behind you and hold your foot or ankle with your hand.

3 Hold for 5 to 10 seconds, then release and repeat on the other side.

4 Repeat twice more on each leg.

2

Standing hamstring (back of thigh) stretch

1 Stand up straight with your knees hip-width apart and your knees soft (slightly bent).

2 Extend one foot forward so that it is pointing in front of you with the weight resting on its heel. Tighten your stomach muscles to protect your back.

3 Rest your hands on the thigh of the bent leg to support your body weight.

4 Bend forward from the hip and feel the stretch in the back of the thigh of the straight leg.

5 Hold for 5 to 10 seconds, then release and repeat on the other side.

6 Repeat twice more on each leg.

4

Train your brain

Use your mind to help you get the most from your workout. Focus on what you are doing correctly. As you are exercising tell yourself how well you are doing. Think of each muscle contracting and stretching as you do your routine. This can make you do even better, whereas concentrating on what you are doing wrong sets you up to fail. You can even use visualizations to convince yourself that your body is becoming fitter and more toned!

GOOD POSTURE

Practise these easy exercises to improve your posture. Remember to keep your movements smooth and flowing throughout.

1

4

Backside tilt

This simple exercise works your hip extensors (gluteus maximus) and is essential for good posture.

1 Stand up straight with your feet hip-width apart and your knees slightly bent. Rest your hands on the top of your hips.

2 Tighten your abdominal muscles by gently pulling in your navel towards your spine – don't suck in your waist or hold your breath.

3 Slowly tilt your pelvis forwards then return to the starting position. The movement should come from your buttocks.

4 Slowly tilt your pelvis backwards then return to the starting position.

Up and down

This is a good exercise for strengthening the quadriceps and for improving your body's alignment. You'll need two small balls for this exercise – tennis balls are ideal.

1 Stand behind a chair and place one ball between your ankles. Place the other ball between your legs just above your knees. Hold on to the chair to keep your balance.

2 Stand up straight with good posture. Slowly rise up on your toes.

3 Slowly come back down again. When your heels are on the floor, gently bend your knees, keeping your heels on the ground. Slowly move up into the starting position.

How to stand properly

Good posture looks relaxed and natural, not hunched or slouched. Stand with your feet hip-width apart. Gently pull up through your legs, keeping your knees slightly bent. Lengthen your spine, pull in your stomach muscles and stand tall. Keep your shoulders down and relaxed so that your neck is as long as possible, and make sure that your weight is distributed evenly over both feet.

WATCH POINT
Don't bend forwards or backwards as you bend your knees.

If you only ever do one type of hip and thigh exercise, make it a squat, which really hits the spot! Squats work the hip extensors, hamstrings (back of thigh muscles) and quadriceps (front of thigh muscles). Tight quads and hamstrings cause poor posture and lower back pain so it's very important to keep them in good working order.

Basic squat

Targeting the buttocks and tops of the thighs, this easy exercise is great for toning up those trouble spots. Remember to keep your knees soft (slightly bent) throughout.

1 Stand up with good posture, your feet hip-width apart and your hands on your hips.

2 Tighten your abdominal muscles by gently pulling your navel towards your spine.

3 Bend your knees and squat as if you were going to sit down. Only squat as far as is comfortable and without losing your balance.

4 Return to the standing position by pushing through your heels, keeping your knees slightly bent as you do so.

3

4

Wide squat

Wide squats are great for toning your inner thigh muscles and the front and back of the thighs. Try not to wobble.

1 Stand up with good posture, your feet wide apart and your toes turned out. Keep your hands on your hips.

2 Tighten your abdominal muscles by gently pulling your navel towards your spine.

3 Bend your knees and lower your bottom as if you were going to sit down.

4 Go as low as you can without wobbling forwards. Return to a standing position by pushing through your heels, keeping your knees slightly bent as you do so.

Single-leg squat

This slightly harder squat really challenges your balance as well as working your hips and thigh muscles.

1 Standing with your feet together and your arms by your sides, shift your weight on to your right foot. Rest the toes of your left foot next to your right foot for balance.

2 Keeping your back straight, bend at the hips and knees and slowly sit back on to your right leg, raising your arms in front of you as you lower. Sit back only as far as is comfortable. Stop and hold for a count of two.

3 Now press into your right foot through the heels and come back up.

4 Repeat the exercise with the weight on your left foot.

2

WATCH POINT
Keep your abdominal
muscles tight
throughout these
exercises.

Lunges are fantastic for firming your hips and thighs, because they work the hip extensors, quadriceps and hamstrings. They're also good exercises to help you improve your balance. When you have become adept at performing lunges, you could hold weights in each hand to increase the workout and you could even do walking lunges, as long as your workout space is big enough, or you are able to turn mid-stride.

Basic lunge

This is a fabulous hip and thigh toner that is extremely versatile because you can hold it for increasing amounts of time. Keep your back straight at all times and keep your movements smooth and fluid.

1 Stand up straight with good posture and your hands on your hips. Tighten your abdominal muscles by gently drawing your navel towards your spine, and tense your buttock muscles.

2 Take a big step forwards. Your back leg should be long and slightly bent at the knee, with the heel off the floor; the front leg should have the knee over the ankle.

3 Dip your lower body down as far as is comfortable. Hold for a count of two.

4 Push your body all the way back up to the standing position using your front leg. Do all your repetitions on one leg then switch legs and repeat on the other side.

WATCH POINT
Don't lunge too deeply – if you let your knee go beyond the line of the end of your toes you will put too much stress on your knee joint.

3

Platform lunge

This is a modified lunge that is great for sculpting the thighs and bottom for a longer, leaner look.

1 Stand up straight with your hands on your hips. Tighten your abdominal muscles to protect your back, and tense your buttock muscles.

2 Take a big step forwards on to a 15–30 cm (6–12 inches) platform. Your back leg should be long and slightly bent at the knee, with the heel off the floor; the front leg should have the knee over the ankle.

3 Dip your lower body down as far as is comfortable.

4 Push back with your front leg to return to a standing position. Do all your repetitions on one leg then switch legs and repeat on the other side.

WATCH POINT
Leaning forwards on the way down puts strain on your back and may cause loss of balance.

SEATED EXERCISES

Even if you're office-bound for a large part of the day or spend a lot of time travelling, you can still sneak in a few exercises to keep your hips and thigh muscles toned. You'll need a straight-backed, sturdy chair for these exercises – not one on castors.

Seated leg extension

This easy exercise is great for toning the quadriceps, the muscles at the front of your thighs. To make this harder, you can use ankle weights to strengthen the intensity of the exercise.

1 Sit up straight with good posture. Tighten your abdominal muscles by pulling in your navel towards your spine – this will protect your back muscles.

2 Press your knees together and straighten one leg. Hold and release. Do all your repetitions on one leg, then repeat on the other leg.

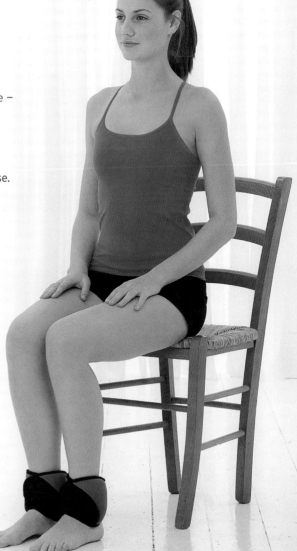

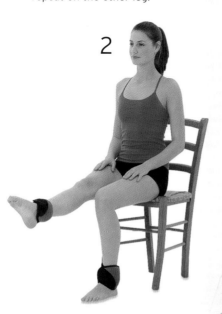

Making the effort

It's important to work at the right intensity if you're aiming to tone up your muscles — if you work out until it hurts you may damage your muscles; put in too little effort and you won't notice any difference. Your muscles should start to become tired during the last repetitions and you may feel a burning sensation, but this is normal and will pass as soon as you rest. Muscle soreness and stiffness is highly likely in the beginning, but if you can hardly move then you've overdone it. Rest up for a day or so and start again at a reduced intensity.

Simple seated thigh squeeze

This tones and strengthens your inner thighs. Make this exercise harder by increasing the time of the squeeze and by using something with more resistance, such as a semi-inflated ball.

1 Sit up straight on a chair with your knees bent and feet together.

2 Place a cushion between your thighs. Squeeze the cushion as hard as possible for a count of five, then release.

As well as tightening up your gluteals, these bridging exercises will help to stabilize your pelvis and your trunk muscles, and work your hamstrings. Take care not to over-arch your back or let it sag, and remember to keep your breathing steady and controlled throughout.

Stability bridge

You need to perfect this exercise in order to improve the stability of the trunk muscles before you can move on to more challenging movements.

1 Lie on your back with your knees bent and your feet flat on the floor, slightly apart. Keep your arms by your sides, palms facing downwards.

2 Tighten your abdominal muscles by gently drawing in your navel towards your spine (which will support your back).

3 Press your lower back down into the floor and gently tilt your pelvis forwards so that the pubic bone rises.

4 Use your hip, thigh and trunk muscles to lift your pelvis until your body forms a straight line from your shoulders to your knees. Hold for a count of five then return to the starting position.

4

3

Bridge squeeze

This buttock-clenching exercise makes the gluteus maximus work to support your back. If you feel a strong contraction in your hamstrings or any strain in your lower back, then you are not using your buttock muscles properly.

1 Lie on your back with your knees bent and feet slightly apart.

2 Tighten your abdominal muscles by gently drawing in your navel towards your spine – (which will protect your back muscles).

3 Curl your bottom off the floor, lifting your pelvis until your knees, hips and chest are in line.

4 Hold this for a count of ten, squeezing your buttock muscles to support the bridge position. Release and repeat.

Types of movement

You will come across the following terms in this book:

ABDUCTION: when you move away from the centre of your body, for example, by raising your leg horizontally in Lateral leg raises.

ADDUCTION: when you move towards the centre of your body, for example, by lowering your leg horizontally in Lateral leg raises.

EXTENSION: straightens a limb or the spine.

FLEXION: bends a limb or the spine.

ROTATION: when your body turns on its axis.

3

Bridge with leg lift

Lifting one leg strengthens the muscles at the back of the buttocks and thighs while increasing balance and control in your stabilizing muscles.

1 Lie on your back with your knees bent and feet slightly apart, and your arms at your sides.

2 Tighten your abdominal muscles by gently drawing in your navel towards your spine.

3 Curl your bottom off the floor, lifting your pelvis until your knees, hips and chest are in line.

4 Extend one leg, lift it level with the knee then lower to the floor. Do all your repetitions on one leg, then repeat on the other leg.

To make this exercise harder, raise your extended leg towards the ceiling, then fold the knee towards your chest and lower your leg back to the starting position. You could also use ankle weights.

Controlling your movements

Make sure that all exercises are performed slowly, carefully, and with your full attention. You really do need to concentrate on what you're doing and think about how your body is responding to any exercise. If an action hurts or you do it too quickly then you're not doing it properly. Movements should flow in a gentle, controlled manner. This enables your muscles to stretch naturally.

4

One-legged buttock clencher

This is a harder exercise that will really work your gluteals.

1 Lie on your back with your knees bent and your feet flat on the floor, slightly apart. Keep your arms by your sides, palms facing downwards.

2 Place your left foot on to your right knee. Tighten your abdominal muscles to support your back.

3 Press your lower back down into the floor and gently tilt your pelvis forwards so that the pubic bone rises. Lift your hips off the floor and squeeze your buttock muscles, then release.

4 Do all your repetitions on one leg then repeat on the other leg.

Buttock walking

This exercise is brilliant for keeping your bottom trim and strengthening the buttock muscles. The floor is a good option because a hard surface is more taxing, but beware of carpet burn, or splinters from old wooden floors.

1 Sit up straight with your legs stretched out in front of you. Cross your arms so that your hands are resting on your shoulders.

2 Breathe in and lengthen your spine. Breathe out, and breathe normally as you 'walk' forwards on your buttocks – ten steps forwards, ten steps back to form one repetition. Repeat as often as you can.

WATCH POINT
Take care not to over-arch your back.

STANDING EXERCISES 2

As well as exercising your hip and thigh muscles, these leg lifts help to improve your balance. You will need to hold on to the back of a chair or a table for support for all these exercises. Keep movements smooth and fluid and move only as far as is comfortable.

Lateral leg raise

This exercise helps to tone and tighten your outer thigh muscles and your hips, as well as improve your balance.

1 Stand up straight with good posture, hands by your sides and feet together, holding on to the back of a chair with both hands for balance.

2 Tighten your abdominal muscles by gently drawing in your navel towards your spine. This will protect your lower back muscles.

3 Raise one leg out to the side about 45 degrees. Keep your toes pointing forwards and hold for a count of three. Relax and do all your repetitions on one leg, then repeat using the other leg.

WATCH POINT
Keep your body straight and both knees soft throughout.

Front leg raise

This exercise strengthens and tones the front of your thighs (quadriceps) and increases your hip flexibility. It also helps with your balance.

1 Stand up straight with your feet together and hold on to the back of a chair sideways with your left hand to balance. Tighten your stomach muscles.

2 With your left leg slightly bent, raise your right leg out in front of you as far as is comfortable. Hold for a count of three.

3 Lower your leg, then do all your repetitions on that leg. Repeat on the other leg.

2

3

Rear leg raise

This strengthens and tones the buttocks, lower back, back of hips and hamstrings. It also helps with your balance. For best results, keep your buttocks tensed throughout – it's harder but better for you in the long run.

1 Stand up straight with your feet together and use your right hand to hold on to the back of a chair sideways to help you balance.

2 Pull in your stomach muscles to support your back and tighten your buttock muscles.

3 Take your right leg back, and touch the floor with your toes. Hold this position for a count of three, then return to the start. Do all your repetitions on one leg, then repeat on the other leg.

These traditional ballet exercises give a great workout to the legs and buttocks. Keep your movements controlled and flowing.

Double knee bends

This exercise, which strengthens your thighs, calves and buttocks, will help you achieve the sculpted legs of a dancer.

1 Stand with your legs a little wider than shoulder-width apart and your feet slightly turned out. Rest your hands on the back of a chair to help you balance.

2 Tighten your abdominal muscles to protect your lower back.

3 Slowly press your knees out and lower yourself down. You should feel this in your bottom and back of your thighs.

4 Return to standing, then tense your buttocks, squeeze your inner thigh muscles and rise up on to your toes. Return to the start position.

3

4

One-legged knee bends

These will strengthen your buttocks, thigh muscles and calves.

1 Stand up with good posture with your right side to the back of a chair and hold on to it for support. Lift and bend your right leg backwards so that the knee faces forwards and your foot is pointing out behind you in line with your knee.

2 Tighten your abdominal muscles to protect your back.

3 Slowly rise up on to the toes of your left foot. Hold for a count of two.

4 Slowly come back down again on to your left foot.

5 Now bend your left knee, bringing the kneecap directly over your foot.

6 Straighten up and repeat five times on the same leg, then do this exercise on the other leg.

Quality control

Focus on perfecting your technique – it's the quality of the movements that will count. Remember to keep your spine aligned and your abdominal muscles pulled in at all times.

3

WATCH POINT
Don't let your bottom stick out.

5

Try these lying-down exercises to work on your thighs and hips. Remember to keep your movements smooth and flowing throughout, and breathe regularly.

Lying kick
This works the hips, bottom and leg muscles.

1 Lie on your left side and bend your left leg beneath you. Support your head with your left hand and put your right hand on the floor in front of you.

2 Tighten your stomach muscles to protect your back and keep your spine in neutral.

3 Slowly bring your right knee up to hip level then slowly push the right leg out straight (but not so that the knee locks). Bend the leg back.

4 Do all your repetitions on one leg then repeat on the other leg.

3

3

Lying inner thigh lift

This is a good one for toning and shaping inner thigh muscles, but don't stretch your legs so wide that your muscles hurt.

1 Lie on your back with your legs straight up in the air.

2 Keep your spine in neutral and tighten your abdominal muscles.

3 Pull your legs out to the sides so that they form a 'V' shape – you will feel a stretch in your inner thigh muscles.

4 Bring your legs together back to the start position.

WATCH POINT

Make sure your spine is in the right position when you are exercising. If you exercise with your pelvis and spine misplaced – either pressed too far into the floor or arched – you may put stress on your lower back and create muscle imbalance.

Scissors

This exercise is fabulous for toning your inner thighs and your stomach muscles.

1 Lie on your back with your legs straight up in the air. Keep your spine in neutral and tighten your abdominal muscles to protect your back.

2 Make a 'V' shape with your legs and then, in a smooth, continuous motion, cross your left leg in front of your right leg, then switch sides in a scissor-like motion.

Exercising on all fours makes your muscles work harder because they're working against gravity. Keep all movements smooth and controlled for best results and don't let your back sag or arch.

Leg lift

This is a lateral thigh raise that works the outer thigh muscles (hip abductors).

1 To start, kneel in the 'box' position (on all fours) and keep your back straight. Tighten your abdominal muscles to support your back.

2 Lift your right leg out to the side – you will feel the muscles at the side of the thigh and hip working to lift your leg. Hold for a count of two.

3 Slowly lower your leg to the start position. Do all your repetitions on one leg, then repeat using the other leg.

Don't exercise if...

- You are feeling unwell – your body will need all its strength to fight off any infection.
- You have an injury – you might make things worse.
- You have an ongoing medical condition or are on medication – consult with your doctor first.
- You've just had a big meal.
- You've been drinking alcohol.

1

2

FLOOR EXERCISES 2

Kneeling kick-back

This works your quadriceps.

1 Get down on all fours and pull in your stomach muscles to protect your back.

2 Raise your right leg off the floor, and with your knee bent, bring it into your body, then stretch it out backwards so that it is in line with your body with the foot flexed.

3 Pull the leg back in and take it back out again. Do all your repetitions on one leg, then repeat using the other leg.

One-hip leg extension

This exercise works the hip extensors (gluteals). To increase the intensity of this exercise, straighten out the leg you are working (but keep the knee soft).

1 Get into the box position and keep your back straight.

2 Tighten your abdominal muscles to protect your back. Tense your buttocks.

3 Lift your right leg upwards with your knee bent and your thigh parallel to the floor.

4 Gently lift your thigh about 5 cm (2 inches) up and then lower again. Lower the leg back to the floor then do all your repetitions on one leg. Repeat the exercise with the other leg.

WATCH POINT
Don't kick back vigorously because this builds up momentum, which can place stress on your lower back muscles.

These side-lying exercises work the abductor muscles at the side of the thighs. Remember to keep your back straight, your hips facing forwards, and breathe regularly throughout.

Outer thigh lift

Make sure you perform each move slowly and in a controlled way to really work the muscles. You don't have to tense your buttocks as you do this but it's good to work your gluteals whenever you can.

1 Lie on your right side with your body in a straight line and your thighs and feet together. Prop yourself up with your right arm and rest your left hand on the floor in front of you. Tighten your stomach muscles by drawing your navel in towards your spine – this will help to protect your back.

2 Bend both knees. Lift up the top leg, then lower, squeezing your buttocks together as you raise and lower your leg.

3 Do all your repetitions on one side then repeat on the other side of your body.

WATCH POINT
Keep the knee of the extended leg soft (slightly bent).

2

Straight-legged outer thigh lift

1 Lie on your side with your lower leg bent and your top leg straight but with the knee soft rather than locked. Your body should be in a straight line and your thighs and knees together. Prop yourself up on your elbow with your head resting on your hand and place the other hand in front of you for support. Keep your stomach muscles pulled in to protect your back.

2 Raise your top leg then lower, squeezing your buttock muscles as you do so. If you are in the correct position you shouldn't be able to lift your leg more than 45 degrees.

3 Do all your repetitions on one side then repeat them on the other side of your body.

2

Keeping up your motivation

All too often people start a new exercise regime burning with enthusiasm, only for it to peter out very quickly to the point where they can't be bothered to do anything at all. When you start your toning programme, be realistic about how and when you can do it. You need to set aside a regular slot for your 6-minute routine so it becomes a natural and automatic part of your everyday routine. But if you do miss several days, don't get disheartened and give up – a little exercise even on a very irregular basis is still better than nothing at all.

These side-lying exercises work your inner thigh muscles (abductors). Remember to keep your spine in neutral and your stomach muscles tightened throughout.

Inner thigh lift

1 Lie on one side with your hips facing forwards and your body in a straight line. Prop yourself up on your elbow with your head resting on your hand and place the other hand on the floor in front of you for support.

2 Tighten your stomach muscles by gently drawing in your navel towards your spine to protect your back.

3 Bend your top leg so that the knee touches the floor in front of you.

4 Raise the bottom extended leg, keeping the knee soft (slightly bent), then lower.

5 Do all your repetitions on one side then repeat them on the other side of your body.

1

4

Straight-legged inner thigh lift

This is a harder exercise, which tones your inner thigh muscles.

1 Lie on your side with your hips facing forwards and your body in a straight line. Prop yourself up on your elbow with your head resting on your hand and place the other hand on the floor in front of you for support.

2 Tighten your stomach muscles by gently drawing in your navel towards your spine to protect your back.

3 Bend your top leg and place the foot flat on the floor just above the knee of the extended leg.

4 Raise your extended leg off the floor as far as you can (this won't be very far) then lower.

5 Do all your repetitions on one side then repeat on the other leg.

Working with your body shape

We all have a unique bone structure and body shape that, frankly, we can't change. Some of us are genetically programmed to be very slender (ectomorphs), others are curvaceous with a tendency to gain weight (endomorphs), while others tend to be athletic (mesomorphs). It's important to work out the shape you are before embarking on your fitness routine – if you are a natural endomorph, no amount of exercise or dieting will give you a waif-like, ectomorphic look. Furthermore, women are naturally designed to store fat on the hips and thighs to protect the reproductive organs – that is, until the menopause, after which they will store fat around the midsection, just like men!

WATCH POINT
Don't raise your bottom leg too high
– you'll over-extend the muscles.

4

STRETCHES

Stretching relieves the muscle tension that is created by exercise and allows the muscles to relax to their full length. This ensures that their full range is used and they do not remain in a semi-contracted state. Stretches help to develop flexibility and keep your body supple and injury-free, and you can perform these at the end of your session, when your muscles are well warmed up.

Lying buttock stretch

This will stretch your buttocks and your outside thigh muscles.

1 Lie on your back and bend your legs. Cross your right ankle over your left knee and lift your left leg off the floor. You will feel a stretch on the outside thigh and buttock of your left leg.

2 Take hold of your left thigh with both hands and slowly draw the left knee in towards you. You will feel the stretch intensify.

3 Hold the stretch for a count of ten. Release and repeat on the other leg.

Lying quad stretch

1 Lie prone (face down) on the floor. Bend one knee and take hold of the foot of that leg with your hand and gently pull the foot towards your buttock.

2 Press your hip down towards the floor (which will ensure you stretch fully the rectus femoris – the quadriceps muscle that crosses the hip joint).

3 Hold the stretch for a count of ten, then release and repeat on the other leg.

Lying hamstring stretch

1 Lie on your back with your knees bent and your feet resting flat on the floor.

2 Lift one leg and grasp the back of the thigh with your hands.

3 Gently pull that leg towards your chest as far as is comfortable. Repeat on the other leg.

Sitting inner thigh stretch

It is very important to stretch the inner thigh (adductor) muscles because they help the quadriceps and hip flexors during running.

1 Sit on the floor with your knees bent and the soles of the feet together, keeping your back straight. Rest your hands on your inner thighs, just above your knees.

2 Use your arms to press downwards to abduct the hip joints and thus stretch the inner thigh muscles as far as is comfortable. Hold for a count of 20, then release.

Top tips for stretching

- Only stretch warm muscles.
- Slowly ease the muscles into position.
- Never bounce into position.
- Do not overstretch — mild discomfort is acceptable but if it hurts, you should stop.
- Breathe freely to enable blood to flow to the muscles — do not hold your breath.

2

Standing hip flexor stretch

You can keep your back knee on the floor for this exercise if you find it difficult to keep your leg straight.

1 Kneel on your right leg, keeping your left leg bent and your left foot firmly on the floor.

2 Put your hands on the floor either side of your left foot to help you balance.

3 Lift your right knee off the floor and straighten the right leg backwards (keeping the knee soft). Dip your pelvis down to the floor as far as is comfortable.

4 Hold for a count of ten, then release and repeat on the other leg.

Sitting outer thigh stretch

1 Sit on the floor with your legs stretched out. Cross the left leg over the right leg, with the left foot flat on the floor on the outer side of the right knee.

2 Rest your left hand on the floor behind your body, with your arm straight to support your upper body.

3 With your right hand, pull your left knee gently over to the right.

4 Hold for a count of ten and feel the stretch in the top of the outer left hip region, then release. Repeat the exercise on the other side.

COOLING DOWN

Cooling down to stretch after your routine helps to loosen any muscles that feel cramped or tight. Cooling-down stretches can be held for longer than ten seconds because the muscles are warm.

Taking it further

The exercises in this book are fine for toning and sculpting your thighs and hips, but if you want to get fit then you'll have to include some activity that raises your heartbeat for at least 15 minutes at a time. Swimming, cycling, fast walking and running are all straightforward options but you could do an exercise class or take up a sport such as tennis – just keep moving and try a variety of activities.

Hip and thigh stretch

1 Kneel with one knee above the ankle and foot flat on the floor, and stretch your other leg behind you so that the knee touches the floor.

2 Place your hands on your front knee to balance yourself. Hold this position for a count of ten, then repeat on the other leg.

2

3

Knee hug

1 Lie on your back with your legs straight. Tighten your abdominal muscles and pull both legs up to your chest.

2 Take hold of your knees and hug your knees tighter to your chest. Hold for a count of ten.

3 Release the pull, then repeat as many times as you wish.

2

Standing full-body stretch

1 Stand tall with your arms by your sides and your feet hip-width apart.

2 Raise your arms above your head and clasp your hands together.

3 Stretch your arms up as high as possible and feel the stretch in your arms, chest, stomach, hips and thighs.

4 Hold for a count of ten, then release.

Here's a simple fortnightly routine for you to follow. Although these are broken down into 6-minute routines, if you're new to exercise don't feel you have to start off doing the whole routine – you can build up the amount of time you spend and the types of exercises you do. You can also make up your own routines. The exercises in this book will tone your hip and thigh muscles within a few weeks but please be aware that they are not for fitness or weight loss.

14-day schedule

The routines below will give your abdominal muscles a good workout. Each routine should take 6 minutes to do, although this may vary depending on the amount of repetitions you do – don't worry if you can't do the full amount at first. The routines also take into account the time it will take for you to get into position and have a short rest between each exercise.

Making the most of your workout

- Always warm up before you begin.
- Think about what you are trying to achieve and be aware of how your body feels as you move.
- Remember to tighten your abdominal muscles.
- Keep your spine aligned.
- Breathe in to prepare and breathe out as you move into position.
- Move slowly and gracefully.
- Cool down at the end to relax and bring your body back to normal.

Day 1

Backside tilt: *1 set (6–8 reps)* **p14**
Basic squat: *1 set (8–12 reps)* **p16**
Front leg raise:
   1 set (8–12 reps) for each leg **p27**
Rear leg raise:
   1 set (8–12 reps) for each leg **p27**
Double knee bends: *1 set (8–12 reps)* **p28**
Lying buttock stretch **p38**
Lying quad stretch **p39**
Lying hamstring stretch **p39**

Day 2

Seated leg extension:
   1 set (10 reps) on each leg **p20**
Simple seated thigh squeeze: *6 reps* **p21**
Stability bridge: *2–4 reps* **p22**
Bridge with leg lift:
   1 set (6–8 reps) on each leg **p24**
Lying kick: *1 set (6–8 reps) on each leg* **p30**
Lying buttock stretch **p38**
Sitting inner thigh stretch **p40**

Day 3

Up and down: *1 set (8–12 reps)* **p15**
Buttock walking: *1 set (8–12 reps)* **p25**
Outer thigh lift: *1 set (6–8 reps)*
 for each leg **p34**
Inner thigh lift: *1 set (6–8 reps) for each leg* **p36**
Lying buttock stretch **p38**
Sitting inner thigh stretch **p40**
Sitting outer thigh stretch **p41**

Day 4

Basic lunge:
 1 set (6–8 reps) for each leg **p18**
Lateral leg raise:
 1 set (10 reps) for each leg **p26**
Front leg raise:
 1 set (8–12 reps) for each leg **p27**
Rear leg raise:
 1 set (8–12 reps) for each leg **p27**
One-legged knee bends:
 1 set (6–8 reps) for each leg **p29**
Lying buttock stretch **p38**
Lying quad stretch **p39**
Lying hamstring stretch **p39**

Day 5

Bridge squeeze: *1 set (6–8 reps)* **p23**
Bridge with leg lift:
 1 set (6–8 reps) for each leg **p24**
Lying kick: *1 set (8–10 reps) for each leg* **p30**
Scissors: *1 set (8–10 reps)* **p31**
Lying buttock stretch **p38**
Sitting inner thigh stretch **p40**
Standing hip flexor stretch **p41**

Day 6

Up and down: *1–2 sets (6–12 reps)* **p15**
Basic squat: *1–2 sets (8–16 reps)* **p16**
Lateral leg raise:
 1–2 sets (10–20 reps) for each leg **p26**
Front leg raise:
 1–2 sets (10–20 reps) for each leg **p27**
Rear leg raise:
 1–2 sets (10–20 reps) for each leg **p27**
Lying buttock stretch **p38**
Lying quad stretch **p39**
Lying hamstring stretch **p39**

Day 7

Backside tilt: *1–2 sets (10–20 reps)* **p14**
Platform lunge:
 1–2 sets (6–12 rep) for each leg **p19**
One-legged knee bends:
 1 set (6–10 reps) for each leg **p29**
Outer thigh lift:
 1 set (6–10 reps) for each leg **p34**
Inner thigh lift:
 1 set (6–10 reps) for each leg **p36**
Lying buttock stretch **p38**
Sitting inner thigh stretch **p40**
Sitting outer thigh stretch **p41**
Standing hip flexor stretch **p41**

Day 8

Up and down: *1–2 sets (8–16 reps)* **p15**
Wide squat: *1 set (8–12 reps)* **p17**
Front leg raise:
  1 set (8–12 reps) for each leg **p27**
Rear leg raise:
  1 set (8–12 reps) for each leg **p27**
One-legged knee bends:
  1 set (8–12 reps) for each leg **p29**
Lying buttock stretch **p38**
Lying quad stretch **p39**
Lying hamstring stretch **p39**

Day 9

Seated leg extension:
  1–2 sets (10–20 reps) on each leg **p20**
Simple seated thigh squeeze:
  1–2 sets (6–12 reps) **p21**
Stability bridge: *1 set (6–10 reps)* **p22**
Bridge with leg lift:
  1 set (6–10 reps) on each leg **p24**
One-legged buttock clencher:
  1 set (6–10 reps) on each leg **p25**
Lying buttock stretch **p38**
Sitting inner thigh stretch **p40**

Day 10

Buttock walking: *1 set (8–12 reps)* **p25**
One-hip leg extension:
  1 set (6–8 reps) on each leg **p33**
Straight-legged outer thigh lift:
  1 set (6–8 reps) on each leg **p35**
Straight-legged inner thigh lift:
  1 set (6–8 reps) on each leg **p37**
Lying buttock stretch **p38**
Sitting outer thigh stretch **p41**
Sitting inner thigh stretch **p40**

Day 11

Platform lunge:
1–2 sets (10–20 reps) for each leg **p19**
Lateral leg raise:
1–2 sets (10–20 reps) for each leg **p26**
Front leg raise:
1–2 sets (10–20 reps) for each leg **p27**
Rear leg raise:
1–2 sets (10–20 reps) for each leg **p27**
One-legged knee bends:
1 set (6–8 reps) for each leg **p29**
Lying buttock stretch **p38**
Lying quad stretch **p39**
Lying hamstring stretch **p39**

Day 12

Bridge squeeze: *1 set (6–8 reps)* **p23**
Bridge with leg lift:
1–2 sets (8–16 reps) on each leg **p24**
One-legged knee bends:
1–2 sets (8–16 reps) on each leg **p29**
Scissors: *2 sets (16–20 reps)* **p31**
Lying buttock stretch **p38**
Sitting inner thigh stretch **p40**
Standing hip flexor stretch **p41**

Day 13

Single-leg squat:
1–2 sets (8–16 reps) on each leg **p17**
Lateral leg raise:
1–2 sets (10–20 reps) on each leg **p26**
Front leg raise:
1–2 sets (10–20 reps) on each leg **p27**
Rear leg raise:
1–2 sets (10–20 reps) on each leg **p27**
Double knee bends: *1–2 sets (6–12 reps)* **p28**
Lying buttock stretch **p38**
Lying quad stretch **p39**
Lying hamstring stretch **p39**

Day 14

Up and down: *1–2 sets (10–20 reps)* **p15**
Platform lunge:
1–2 sets (8–16) on each leg **p19**
One-legged knee bends:
1 set (6–10 reps) on each leg **p29**
Straight-legged outer thigh lift:
1 set (6–10 reps) on each leg **p35**
Straight-legged inner thigh lift:
1 set (6–10 reps) on each leg **p37**
Lying buttock stretch **p38**
Sitting inner thigh stretch **p40**
Standing hip flexor stretch **p41**

INDEX